REMARKABLE REPTILES

ALLIGATORS

James E. Gerholdt

Published by Abdo & Daughters, 4940 Viking Drive, Suite 622, Edina, Minnesota 55435.

Library bound edition distributed by Rockbottom Books, Pentagon Tower, P.O. Box 36036, Minneapolis, Minnesota 55435.

Printed in the United States.

Cover Photo credit: Natural Selection
Interior Photo credits: James Gerholdt pages 4, 5, 10, 14
        Natural Selection pages 6, 8, 9, 12, 16-19
        Stock Market pages 7, 15, 21
        Peter Arnold pages 11, 13, 20

Edited By Julie Berg

LIBRARY OF CONGRESS CATALOGING-IN-PUBLICATION DATA

Gerholdt, James E., 1943-
  Alligators / James E. Gerholdt
    p. cm. -- (Remarkable Reptiles)
  Includes index.
  ISBN 1-56239-309-X
  1. Alligators -- Juvenile literature. 2. Crocodiles--Juvenile
literature. [1. Alligators. 2. Crocodiles.] I. Title.
  II. Series: Gerholdt, James E., 1943- Remarkable Reptiles.
  QL666.C925G475   1994
  597.98--dc20   94-14053
                    CIP
                    AC

CONTENTS

ALLIGATORS and CROCODILES

Alligators and crocodiles are reptiles. Reptiles are ectothermic. This means they get their body temperature from the environment, either by lying in the sun on a sandbar or the edge of a lake or river. Alligators have a short blunt nose, and the fourth tooth on the lower jaw fits inside the upper jaw. Crocodiles usually have a sharp pointed nose and the fourth tooth on the lower jaw fits outside the upper jaw. There are 22 species in the world. Many species are endangered because of habitat loss and the fact that their skins make nice leather.

This American crocodile is warming itself in the sun.

The fourth tooth on the lower jaw of this alligator fits inside its upper jaw.

The fourth tooth on the lower jaw of this crocodile fits in a notch outside its upper jaw.

SIZES

Some alligators are huge. The biggest American alligator ever found was more than 19 feet long. But the Chinese alligator only reaches a length of 6 feet. Crocodiles can be even larger. The Saltwater crocodile has been found over 20 feet long, as have the American and Orinoco crocodiles. The smallest of all the alligators and crocodiles is the Congo dwarf crocodile. This species doesn't even grow to 4 feet long! The average length of all species ranges from 3 feet to about 15 feet.

These are American alligators, which are some of the largest in the world.

This is a Dwarf crocodile from Australia.

SHAPES

All alligators and crocodiles become very large around when they grow up. The difference in their shapes is in their head. The alligators and South American caiman have short blunt noses. A few crocodiles also have short blunt noses. But most of them have long slender noses. The False gavial from southeast Asia and the Gharial from India have the longest noses of all.

This Florida alligator has a short, blunt snout.

The Indian Gavial has a long slender snout.

COLORS

Alligators and crocodiles have colors that help them blend in with their surroundings. This is called camouflage. Sometimes what looks like a log in the water will come to life and swim away! The brightest of all the crocodiles is the Cuban crocodile. But even its bright colors blend in. Male and female alligators and crocodiles have the same colors. Often the back of one of these reptiles will be covered with algae. While this might be a bright green color, it actually helps them blend in.

These young Cuban crocodiles are brightly colored.

This American alligator appears to be covered with algae.

HABITAT

All alligators and crocodiles live in the water. Each species has its own special habitat. Some live along rivers while others like swamps or the edges of lakes. One kind, the Saltwater crocodile, even swims out to sea. But no matter what exact kind of habitat it lives in, each species must have water deep enough to escape to and an area to get out of the water so it can lie in the sun.

Alligators like to sun themselves but they are never too far from water which keeps them cool.

This young Caiman crocodile enjoys muddy water.

SENSES

Alligators and crocodiles have the same 5 senses as humans. All of them have very good eyesight, and they have a membrane that closes over the eye to protect it when they are underwater. Their hearing is also very good, when the ears are out of the water. Both the nostrils and the ears close when they are under the water. The eyes and the nostrils are set high on the head so the animal can see and breathe when they are floating at the surface of the water.

Alligators have very good eyesight.

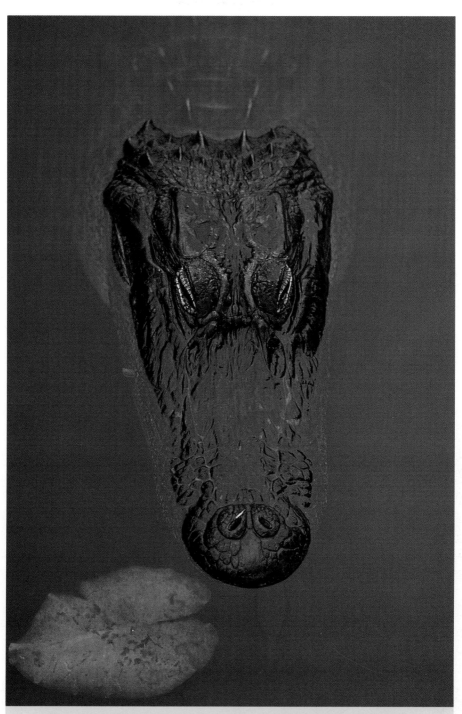

The eyes and ears of the alligator are high up on the head allowing the animal to float just below the surface of the water.

DEFENSE

The most important defense of alligators and crocodiles is
their camouflage. If they are lying in the sun they will escape
into the water at the first sign of danger and submerge themselves.
They can also run fast! An alligator or crocodile runs with its
body off of the ground. Another defense is the tail. An alligator
or crocodile can use it to hit an enemy with a lot of power. Of
course, with huge jaws and teeth, they can also bite.

The tail of an alligator is very powerful.

Their most fearsome weapon is their powerful jaws.

FOOD

Alligators and crocodiles eat insects, frogs, turtles, fish, birds, and mammals. Sometimes they eat people! If they find a dead animal in the water, they will eat it also. One way they catch their food is to ambush it. They will lie in the water, looking like a floating log. When an animal comes to the water to drink, they will grab it with their jaws and pull it into the water and drown it. They spin their body with the animal in their mouth. This is called a "death roll".

This crocodile has an egret in its mouth.

This alligator is waiting in the water to catch its dinner.

BABIES

Of all the reptiles, alligators and crocodiles are the best parents. All 22 species lay eggs. Some dig a hole in the sand for the eggs. This is called a hole nest. Others actually build a nest out of rotting vegetation. This is called a mound nest. The nest is guarded by the female, and occasionally by the male. After 2 months the eggs begin to hatch. As the babies hatch, they call with a high pitched grunting noise. This tells the mother that it is time to dig up the nest. The babies aren't able to dig their way to the surface alone. Often the babies are carried to the water in their mother's mouth. Sometimes the father helps. The babies are guarded by the parents for up to 2 years.

This mother alligator is carrying her baby in her mouth.

These baby alligators are running for water.
Their parents are probably close by.

GLOSSARY

Algae (AL-gee) - A plant without a stem that lives in the water.

Camouflage (CAM-o-flaj) - The ability to blend in with the surroundings.

Ectothermic (ek-to-THERM-ik) - Regulating body temperature from an outside source.

Endangered (en-DAIN-jerd) - At risk of extinction.

Environment (en-VI-ron-ment) - Surroundings an animal lives in.

Habitat (HAB-e-tat) - An area an animal lives in.

Reptiles (REP-tiles) - Scaly skinned animals with backbones.

Vegetation (vej-e-TAY-shun) - Plants found in an area.

Index

About the Author

Jim Gerholdt has been studying reptiles and amphibians for more than 40 years. He has presented lectures and displays throughout the state of Minnesota for 9 years. He is a founding member of the Minnesota Herpetological Society and is active in conservation issues involving reptiles and amphibians in India and Aruba, as well as Minnesota.

Photo by Tim Judy